EXPLORING CIVIL RIGHTS

THE BEGINNINGS
1939

JAY LESLIE

Franklin Watts®
An imprint of Scholastic Inc.

Content Consultant

A special thank you to Ryan M. Jones at the National Civil Rights Museum for his expert consultation.

Library of Congress Cataloging-in-Publication Data
Names: Leslie, Jay, author.
Title: The beginnings : 1939 / by Jay Leslie.
Other titles: Exploring civil rights.
Description: New York : Franklin Watts, an imprint of Scholastic Inc.,
    [2022]. | Series: Exploring civil rights | Includes bibliographical
    references and index. | Audience: Ages 10–14 | Audience: Grades 7–9 |
    Summary: "Series continuation. Narrative nonfiction, key events of the
    Civil Rights Movement in the years spanning from 1939–1954. Photographs
    throughout"— Provided by publisher.
Identifiers: LCCN 2022002626 (print) | LCCN 2022002627 (ebook) |
    ISBN 9781338800531 (library binding) | ISBN 9781338800548 (paperback) |
    ISBN 9781338800555 (ebk)
Subjects: LCSH: African Americans—Civil rights—History—Juvenile
    literature. | Civil rights movements--United States—History—20th
    century—Juvenile literature. | Civil rights workers—United
    States—Juvenile literature. | BISAC: JUVENILE NONFICTION / History /
    United States / 20th Century | JUVENILE NONFICTION / History / United
    States / General
Classification: LCC E185.61 .L5175 2022 (print) | LCC E185.61 (ebook) |
    DDC 323.1196/073—dc23/eng/20220131
LC record available at https://lccn.loc.gov/2022002626
LC ebook record available at https://lccn.loc.gov/2022002627

10 9 8 7 6 5 4 3 2 1   23 24 25 26 27

Printed in China   62
First edition, 2023

Composition by Kay Petronio

COVER & TITLE PAGE: Marian Anderson sings on the steps of the Lincoln Memorial in April 1939.

Mary McLeod Bethune, page 13.

Table of Contents

INTRODUCTION
The Way It Was 4

1 Black America's New Deal 8

2 The Fight for Civil Liberties 18

3 Our Country, 'Tis of Thee 28

4 Caring for a Nation 42

5 A New Chapter for the NAACP 54

6 War in Europe 66

CONCLUSION
The Legacy of 1939 in Civil Rights History 80

Biography STACEY ABRAMS 84
Timeline 88
Glossary 90
Bibliography 92
Index 94
About the Author 96

Thurgood Marshall, page 58.

African American students sit in a segregated classroom during the Jim Crow era in the late 1800s.

The Way It Was

In the period directly following the American Civil War (1861–1865), three **amendments** to the U.S. Constitution sought to grant African Americans the rights they'd been denied during slavery. In 1865, the Thirteenth Amendment abolished slavery. In 1868, the Fourteenth Amendment granted **citizenship** to African Americans. And in 1870, the Fifteenth Amendment gave African American men the right to vote.

Despite those triumphs, this period also saw the introduction of Black codes, or laws passed to limit the rights and freedoms of Black Americans. They soon became known as **Jim Crow** laws, and they were especially strict in the American South. Jim Crow laws controlled where people of color could live and work.

Jim Crow laws enforced **segregation**. Under the racial policy of "separate but equal," Black Americans could be given separate facilities if the quality was equal to the white facilities. In reality, however, there was no equality. African Americans were forced to attend separate and inadequate schools, live in run-down neighborhoods, and even drink from rusty or broken public water fountains.

In 1896, a group of **activists** tried to overturn the Jim Crow laws with the U.S. Supreme Court case *Plessy v. Ferguson*. Unfortunately, when the case was lost, Jim Crow laws became even more acceptable across the country, but remained most common in the southern United States.

The Fight Begins

As Jim Crow expanded, two prominent **civil rights** organizations emerged. The National Association of Colored Women's Clubs (NACWC) was founded in 1896 by a group of politically active women, including Harriet Tubman. Members of the association dedicated themselves to fighting for voting rights and for ending racial violence in the form of **lynchings** against African Americans. In addition to lynchings, African Americans suffered severe harassment, beatings, and even bombings at the hands of racist organizations like the **Ku Klux Klan** (KKK), which had millions of members by the 1920s.

The National Association for the Advancement of Colored People (NAACP), founded in 1909, followed in the NACWC's footsteps. The NAACP focused on opposing segregation and Jim Crow policies. Both organizations would be crucial in the coming fight for justice.

Many African Americans find themselves kicked out of their homes during the Great Depression.

1939

The year 1939 was one of constant change in the United States. The decade-long **Great Depression** left millions of African American families in poverty. A group of Black activists and attorneys, who would become known as the Black Cabinet, began providing direction and advice to the president. The Department of Justice Civil Liberties Unit (CLU) and the NAACP Legal Defense Fund successfully brought Jim Crow cases to court for the first time in American history. And the nation listened as the Black opera singer Marian Anderson triumphantly helped the country come together with her voice. Finally, the outbreak of World War II forced Americans to make a tough choice between fighting for freedom overseas or at home. ∎

President Franklin Delano Roosevelt delivers the State of the Union Address on January 4, 1939.

1

Black America's New Deal

Inequality, both at home in the United States and overseas in Europe, was on President Franklin D. Roosevelt's mind when he delivered that year's State of the Union Address on January 4, 1939. The State of the Union Address is a speech the U.S. president must deliver to Congress at the start of each year to let members know what is happening in the country and recommend new laws and policies for solving the nation's problems.

Across the Atlantic, **Nazi** Germany was growing more powerful and more dangerous by the day. The Nazis were a racist political party that believed white Germans were superior to all other peoples, particularly Jews. A second world war was on the horizon; Americans could feel it. They worried that Nazi German soldiers would soon arrive on the shores of the United States. During the State of the Union, Roosevelt assured Americans that, if necessary, their country would fight to protect freedom and democracy in America—but only in self-defense.

The second issue President Roosevelt wanted to address was the Great Depression. The Great Depression was a financial crisis that left millions of Americans poor and out of work. It began in 1929; by 1939, the country had been deep in the Depression for a decade.

To counter the Great Depression, Roosevelt had begun many government programs called the New Deal, that employed people of *all* races. During his 1939 speech, he urged Americans to stay strong. Although his programs had created millions of jobs, millions more Americans remained unemployed. They did not always have enough food on the table. But if

everyone stuck together, he said, they would be able to get through the crisis. The end was in sight.

The Black Cabinet

On January 13, the second National Conference on Problems of the Negro and Negro Youth took place. This was a gathering of Black and white activists concerned about issues facing Black Americans; they were joined at the conference by members of President Roosevelt's Black Cabinet.

The Black Cabinet, which was also called the Federal Council of Negro Affairs, was a group of 45 African Americans who advised Roosevelt on political and policy matters during his presidency. The Black Cabinet lasted from 1933 to 1945 and its members were the first African American advisers to give counsel to a president. The group fought to make sure that African Americans were fairly included in all

Members of the Black Cabinet meet to advise President Roosevelt.

Unemployed African American men line up to participate in the New Deal in 1933.

government policies. This was crucial because African Americans were largely underrepresented in elected positions. Although the Fifteenth Amendment promised Black men the right to vote, this right was denied in many parts of the country. That meant the Black Cabinet was, for many African Americans, the only way their voices would be heard in the **federal** government.

The Great Depression

The Black Cabinet worked with Roosevelt to help Black Americans through the Great Depression. African Americans were the hardest-hit group of people during this period because **discrimination** made it hard for them to find employment. They were often the "last hired, first fired" for jobs. The unemployment rate for Black citizens was two to three times higher than that of white Americans.

Mary McLeod Bethune

Born in 1875 to parents who had once been enslaved, Mary McLeod Bethune dedicated her life to serving the public as a civil rights activist. As a member of the Black Cabinet, she advised President Roosevelt on issues affecting millions of African Americans. She founded Bethune-Cookman University, one of many private Black universities that were necessary when few universities admitted African Americans, and she served as a leader in the Women's Army Auxiliary Corps, a U.S. military branch for women. She was also active in the fight for international human rights. In 1945, she was the only African American woman to help create the United Nations charter, an agreement bringing together countries from all over the world. Because of her dedication to civil rights, Bethune was often called "The First Lady of the Struggle."

Mary McLeod Bethune (left) shakes hands with young students in 1939.

As part of the New Deal, Roosevelt had begun a series of government jobs programs called the Works Progress Administration, or the WPA. These were public works projects that brought jobs to millions of American construction workers and artists, like writers and musicians.

The Black Cabinet aimed to make sure that African Americans received a fair percentage of the government benefits and jobs available through the New Deal. This provided millions of African American families with financial stability for the first time in a decade.

Lynching

At the January 13 National Conference, First Lady Eleanor Roosevelt addressed the evil problem of lynching.

Lynching is the killing of a person by a mob, typically by hanging. The majority of lynchings committed in the United States were carried out by large white mobs against African American men. Lynchings were violent and brutal.

Between 1930 and 1938, 126 Black people were known to have been lynched in the United States, but this problem had persisted for over a century. And for over a century, the U.S. government had done very little to stop the lynchings.

Only the U.S. federal government had the ultimate

authority to prevent lynching nationwide, by making it a federal crime. Outraged by the number of victims, Eleanor Roosevelt publicly supported the idea of a federal bill to **criminalize** lynching. The first lady pleaded for the federal government to pass a law to end this vicious practice.

However, despite his wife's good intentions, President Roosevelt declined to support a federal anti-lynching bill. He did not want to lose the support of southern legislators whose votes he needed for other government programs. Many southern legislators held racist views and did not oppose lynching or other forms of violence against African Americans. Without the president's pressure, an anti-lynching bill had no chance of passing in Congress.

Social Insecurity

Lynching threatened the lives of African Americans all over the country. At the same time, **Social Security** failed to protect their livelihoods.

First Lady Eleanor Roosevelt proposes an anti-lynching campaign at the National Conference.

The federal Social Security program, started in 1935, provided much-needed financial benefits to retired workers. However, its policies excluded workers employed in agriculture or as **domestic** help, two fields that primarily employed African Americans.

This meant that during the Depression, African American families could not receive the same financial aid as white families and sank further into poverty.

On January 30, 1939, Social Security coverage was extended to married women and to women whose husbands had died. While this was a victory for women, the policy still excluded farm workers and domestic help—and therefore overlooked countless African Americans. Neither group was able to receive these benefits until 1950. ■

An African American sharecropper works on fields in Louisiana.

An African American domestic worker takes care of a white child.

African American Women in the Great Depression

During the Great Depression, the most secure jobs for women were in teaching, cleaning, and other low-paying positions considered "women's work." The number of women in the workforce rose 24 percent between 1930 and 1940, as large numbers of white women sought work while their husbands remained unemployed.

Although white women were new to the workforce, African American women were not. This was because lower wages for African American men meant that very few Black households could survive on just one person's income. With the Great Depression surge of white women into positions like domestic work—positions normally held by African American women—it became even more difficult for Black women to find employment.

Frank Murphy establishes the Civil Liberties Unit to fight for the rights of minorities.

2

The Fight for Civil Liberties

The goal of the U.S. Department of Justice (DOJ) is to make sure that everyone within the country's borders are treated fairly and equally. In practice, however, the DOJ's protection during the Jim Crow era often applied only to white Americans. This department rarely sought justice for African Americans, even though African Americans made up nearly a tenth of the population and faced extensive discrimination in the United States.

Fighting for the rights of African Americans often seemed like a lost cause. Jim Crow laws remained in full effect in the South, and discrimination throughout the rest of the country was common and widespread. African Americans had very few legal rights in court. In California, for example, they couldn't even **testify** against white people.

Frank Murphy believed that justice should be extended to *everyone*. He had no idea how difficult it would be to achieve this goal. Murphy was a young, white lawyer who had just been appointed U.S. attorney general by President Roosevelt. The U.S. attorney general heads the DOJ and holds the highest legal office in the country.

In early February, Murphy established the Civil Liberties Unit (CLU). The CLU had several goals. The unit wanted to reexamine the Thirteenth, Fourteenth, and Fifteenth Amendments so that lawyers could **prosecute** more human rights cases. The unit wanted to push for fairer labor laws and enforce voting rights. And the unit wanted to be able to prosecute officials such as police officers and sheriffs, not just private citizens.

These were challenging goals, for nothing like them had ever been attempted at the federal level.

African Americans line up to register to vote in Atlanta, Georgia.

Activists from across the country protest against lynching.

The Law and Civil Liberties

The CLU faced one major obstacle after another. Although its aim was to fight for every form of justice possible, it could pursue only injustices that had already taken place.

The CLU also wanted to target racist individuals and institutions in the South, where Jim Crow was the law of the land, and discrimination was the most open and obvious. Southern politicians, for example, knew it was illegal to ban African Americans from voting in general elections. However, they could legally ban Black Americans from voting in the primary elections. In a primary election, voters decide between

African Americans gather outside a court-house to witness the trial of 31 white men who lynched a Black man.

candidates within the same political party. The winner of the primary election will then be that political party's candidate in the general election. By blocking Black citizens from voting in primary elections, southern politicians ensured that African Americans had no say in choosing who ran for office.

Another problem faced by the CLU was not being trusted by the African American community since it was so new. After all, for hundreds of years, the U.S. government had denied their rights. Why did the government suddenly claim to want to help them?

As a result, those whose rights had been violated rarely came forward—they didn't trust the CLU's lawyers enough to seek their help.

No Crime Committed

When African Americans did bring cases to the CLU, its lawyers faced another major obstacle. Victims and witnesses were too scared to testify in court.

Usually, the victim was an African American man who had been beaten, tortured, or driven out of town. The victim knew that making his story public would only lead to further physical abuse.

For similar reasons, African Americans who had witnessed a crime often declined to come forward, fearing for their own safety. They knew that, despite the CLU's good intentions, the unit couldn't protect witnesses from being physically assaulted after taking the stand in court. And even if evidence was gathered, there was no guarantee that the CLU could successfully take the case to a real trial.

African Americans appear in court before two white men in Virginia.

It was up to a grand jury to decide whether a case could actually go to trial. A grand jury is a group of 16–23 citizens who determine whether there is enough evidence to charge an accused person with a crime. Unfortunately, members of the jury were often **prejudiced**. In civil rights cases, more often than not, the grand jury decided that a crime had not been committed and the charges were dropped. Overall, the chances of getting justice were very slim. For many Black Americans, the safest thing to do was to try to live life as quietly as possible.

The seal for the U.S. Department of Justice.

Earning Trust

The CLU refused to back down. The unit partnered with the Federal Bureau of Investigation (FBI) to gather as many witnesses as possible for each case. It began sending representatives from the federal government into the South to make sure court proceedings were following the law. The CLU also made itself more well known in Black communities so that African Americans no longer saw its lawyers as strangers.

Slowly, the CLU began to win the trust of those whom it wanted to protect. In 1957, the unit would be expanded and renamed the Civil Rights Division of the Department of Justice. ▪

The *Amistad* Mutiny

On July 2, 1839, the Spanish slave ship *La Amistad* was sailing from one port in Cuba to another when the enslaved Africans on board took control of the ship. It was a **mutiny**. One of the enslaved men, Joseph Cinqué, broke free of his shackles and led the other 52 in an uprising. They overthrew the captain and demanded that the ship's Spanish navigator sail them back to their home in Africa. The navigator agreed. But instead, he sailed the boat to New York.

Joseph Cinqué, leader of *La Amistad* slave uprising.

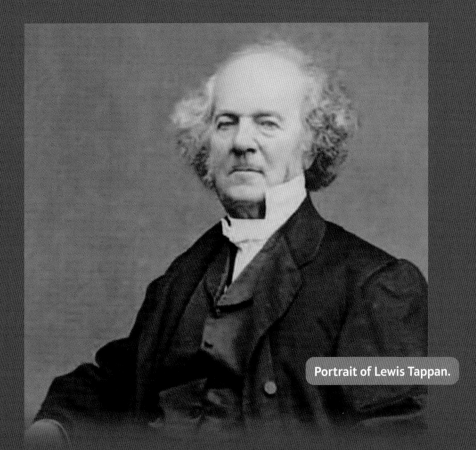

Portrait of Lewis Tappan.

In New York, the U.S. government took control of the ship, and President Martin Van Buren had the Africans imprisoned while he decided what to do with them. Van Buren, who was up for reelection soon, wanted to win votes among southern slaveholders by sending the captives back to Cuba in chains.

However, activist and lawyer Lewis Tappan fought for the enslaved men in a federal court. He argued that because it was illegal to bring slaves into the United States, these men weren't actually slaves—they were free people who had been kidnapped. Therefore, their mutiny was justified, and they had the right to go free. Tappan won the case.

Cinqué and the other enslaved men returned home to Africa in January 1842.

African American soldiers march through France during World War I.

3

Our Country, 'Tis of Thee

Pursuing acts of **voter suppression** and criminal justice was just a small part of the battle for civil rights.

Within the armed forces, African Americans weren't only fighting for their country. Like much of the United States as a whole, the U.S. military was strictly segregated. White and Black soldiers fought in separate units, and Black soldiers were not allowed to become officers. They were not allowed to serve in the Army Air Corps (now called the Air Force).

Twenty years earlier, between 1917 and 1918, some 350,000 African Americans had laid their lives on the line to fight in World War I. In addition to the enemy, they also faced discrimination within their own military. Black soldiers were often forced to sleep outside in tents while white soldiers slept in warm barracks. Denied proper gear, some African American soldiers were given old uniforms and didn't get a change of clothes for months at a time. While white soldiers fought in combat positions, Black soldiers were limited to jobs that white soldiers didn't want to do, such as digging trenches, burying soldiers who had been killed in battle, and removing explosives from fields.

Since World War I, African American members of the military had been actively campaigning for equal rights in the armed forces. Some wanted full **integration**, while others accepted segregation as long as they earned equal pay and were eligible to become officers.

African American soldiers build a railroad in France during World War I.

Now, in the spring of 1939, as the power of Nazi Germany continued to spread steadily across Europe, it became increasingly clear that another world war was coming. African Americans wanted to serve in this war. But if they were going to fight for America, they wanted to be treated fairly.

African American members of the military began sending letters to the War Department, demanding equal rights. Soon other Americans also began writing letters. Members of the NAACP, journalists, World War I veterans, citizens who wanted to enlist, and officers of the National Guard flooded the War Department with thousands of letters demanding changes in the military.

In response, President Roosevelt and Congress approved a bill known as Public Law 18. The law went into effect on April 2, 1939, and allowed African Americans to receive training and admission to the Air Corps for the first time in U.S. history. It would take four more years for the first African American airmen to finally be deployed, but the law was a start.

An Easter to Remember

On April 9, 1939, Easter Sunday, many Americans took a break from worrying about the war and the Great Depression to celebrate the holiday with their families. Across the country, millions of Americans

eagerly tuned their radios to hear a very special performance.

Opera singer Marian Anderson was nervous. She peeked anxiously out at the audience gathered in Washington, DC, to hear her. Every time she looked, the crowd seemed to be growing bigger and bigger and buzzing with more excitement.

That evening, the audience swelled to 10,000, then 20,000, then 50,000. By the time she took the stage, 75,000 people were packed on the steps of the Lincoln Memorial and onto the National Mall for one reason: to hear her sing.

Anderson had been a professional singer for more than 10 years. She had entertained thousands of fans

across the United States and Europe. She had head-
lined in theaters and concert halls in France, the Soviet
Union, and Spain.

But those performances were nothing compared
to this one. In the United States, African American
singers were often banned from large, white-only
spaces and were almost never given the spotlight. So
that day, Anderson wasn't representing only herself.
She was representing all the African American artists
who were denied the opportunity to perform. She felt
the pressure to deliver a perfect performance. She was
nervous because of what her historic performance
would mean for segregation and the future of African
American artists in the United States.

Anderson tried not to let her nerves show. "I could not run away from this situation. If I had anything to offer, I would have to do so now," she said later. But the road to get here had been long and difficult, and many people did not want her to sing that day.

A Magical Voice

Born in 1897, Anderson began singing at age six. Her voice was enchanting. Everyone who heard her knew that she had a special gift.

She was so talented that she began earning money by singing when she was still a child. But her young music career stalled when tragedy struck. Her father died when she was just 12 years old.

After his death, her family could no longer afford to give her music lessons. They couldn't even send her to high school. Anderson had to drop out of school to take care of her younger sisters while her mother worked. With no way forward, it seemed as though Anderson would be forced to give up the chance to have a singing career.

Nevertheless, she persevered, practicing on her own and performing whenever she could. In 1921, she tried to enroll at the famous Philadelphia Musical Academy. She knew she had the talent for it; she just needed someone to believe in her.

The white woman working in admissions denied her entry.

Discouraged but not defeated, in 1925 Anderson entered a singing competition at the New York Philharmonic, one of the oldest and most respected musical institutions in the country. She won!

A New Start

Sponsored by a music program, Anderson moved to Europe, where she was surprised to find that racism didn't exist as it did in the United States. For the first time in her life, white people treated her as an equal. When she performed during a tour across Europe, every audience cheered, and people everywhere praised her.

As much as she enjoyed touring, her heart and her family were in the United States. So in 1935, she returned to the East Coast. The difference between Europe and America was stark. Jim Crow laws prevented her from singing on most stages or staying in most hotels. Most white people didn't care that she was famous. To them, she was just another Black American.

Despite segregation, however, it was hard for crowds of any color to deny that Anderson had an incredible singing voice, and her fame in the United States steadily grew.

Anderson planned to perform a concert for the public on Easter Sunday, 1939, at Constitution Hall.

African Americans in Europe

Like Marian Anderson, many African American artists sought more freedom in Europe. Europe allowed Black artists to pursue their passions and receive training without the racial discrimination and segregation they faced in the United States. France was a particularly popular option. An artistic movement in France arose from global Black unity among Africans, African Americans, and Afro-Europeans.

Composer and band leader Duke Ellington in France in 1939.

Daughters of the American Revolution gather in Constitution Hall, where they forbid Marian Anderson from performing.

Thousands of fans were expected, and Constitution Hall is still the largest concert hall in Washington, DC.

Like many places in the South, Constitution Hall was segregated. Black audience members had to squeeze into a small, cramped area of the balcony.

Marian Anderson didn't agree with this policy, but she was used to it. However, the hall was owned by the Daughters of the American Revolution (DAR), a historical society comprised of white women whose ancestors fought in the Revolutionary War. Their policy was that only white people were allowed to perform onstage. Despite Anderson's fame, they would not allow her to sing on their stage.

The First Lady Intervenes

When Eleanor Roosevelt, a member of the DAR, heard that Anderson had been banned from Constitution Hall, she was outraged.

She tried to use her position as first lady to call attention to this **bigotry**. She hadn't been able to stop lynching, but perhaps she could at least give Anderson and other African American singers the public platform they deserved. So the first lady resigned from the DAR in a public letter. She also wrote about the issue in her weekly newspaper column, "My Day."

But the DAR refused to budge. Even though the first lady called national attention to its bigotry, the organization refused to let Anderson sing.

February 28, 1939.

Henry M.

My dear Mrs. Robert: Jr.

I am afraid that I have never been a very useful member of the Daughters of the American Revolution, so I know it will make very little difference to you whether I resign, or whether I continue to be a member of your organization.

However, I am in complete disagreement with the attitude taken in refusing Constitution Hall to a great artist. You have set an example which seems to me unfortunate, and I feel obliged to send in to you my resignation. You had an opportunity to lead in an enlightened way and it seems to me that your organization has failed.

I realize that many people will not agree with me, but feeling as I do this seems to me the only proper procedure to follow.

Very sincerely yours,

Letter sent by Eleanor Roosevelt to the Daughters of the American Revolution.

38

"Strange Fruit"

On April 20, 1939, African American singer Billie Holiday recorded "Strange Fruit," a song originally written as a poem by Abel Meeropol, an American Jew, to protest the lynchings in the American South. The song reminded Holiday of her father, who died at the age of 39 due to a lack of medical treatment for a lung condition. He was turned away from a hospital for being Black.

This became a protest song, and activists even mailed their senators copies of the record to persuade them to publicly oppose racial injustice.

Billie Holiday sings in Chicago in 1939.

Marian Anderson sings on the steps of the Lincoln Memorial on Easter Sunday in 1939.

Of Thee "We" Sing

Now that the first lady was involved, the federal government couldn't simply turn a blind eye. It needed to find a solution that would be appropriate for someone of Anderson's fame and would show support for the African American singer.

The Roosevelt administration settled on the open-air steps of the Lincoln Memorial. The site would be large enough for an audience of thousands. Moreover, President Abraham Lincoln had written the 1863 Emancipation Proclamation announcing the end of slavery.

That day, at dusk, Anderson opened with a very special song: the patriotic "My Country, 'Tis of Thee," an ode to America.

At the third line of the song, "Of thee I sing," she sang instead, "Of thee *we* sing," calling together all members of the audience.

The integrated crowd was enormous, stretching all the way from the Lincoln Memorial to the Washington Monument, nearly a mile away. Many sang along. Millions more listened to the concert on the radio. The performance was such a success that it boosted Anderson's international fame. In 1955, she became the first African American to perform at the Metropolitan Opera in New York City. ■

The Federal Surplus Commodities Corporation hands out cabbage and potatoes to hungry Americans in 1938.

4

Caring for a Nation

Marian Anderson briefly brought the country together. Most Americans listened to the Easter broadcast with hearts full of hope. Unfortunately, many of their stomachs were still empty. Millions of Americans remained unemployed due to the Great Depression. Many couldn't afford to buy groceries. Farmers had plenty of crops but no one to buy them. As families starved, the farmers destroyed their crops, unable to sell them.

This infuriated Americans who had nothing to eat. To put food on their plates, an agency of the federal government called the Federal Surplus Commodities Corporation gathered the crops that the farmers were going to destroy and gave them away for free at places across the country. This was helpful for hungry families, but it spelled disaster for the farmers, who could no longer sell *any* crops: People could now just wait for the government to give food away for free.

President Roosevelt needed to think of something else.

Henry A. Wallace, the head of the Department of Agriculture, and **economist** Milo Perkins had an idea. They called it the Food Stamp Program (FSP).

On May 16, the program launched. The FSP sold special coupons that allowed people to buy large amounts of food cheaply. For example, people who paid $1 received coupons that let them buy $1.50 worth of food.

This was especially crucial for African Americans, since one out of every four African Americans needed government assistance. And thanks to Roosevelt's policies and support from the Black Cabinet, the government was willing to provide it.

Coupon from the Food Stamp Program, 1939.

An American Hero

Food stamps meant that Black and white families alike could finally afford to put food on their tables during the Depression. In that way, the FSP was an equalizer. There weren't very many other policies in the United States where Black and white people were treated as equals.

Sports like football and baseball were also divided along a color line, but in the boxing ring, spectators

A poor sharecropper family in Missouri does not have much to eat for Thanksgiving in 1939.

liked to see blood; they didn't care whose blood it was. And in 1939, Joe Louis, nicknamed the "Brown Bomber," had been the heavyweight champion of the world for two years.

One year earlier, Nazi Germany was rapidly expanding its power throughout Europe. In March 1938, Germany took the nearby country of Austria under its control and clearly planned to do the same with other countries. So when Joe Louis faced off against German boxer Max Schmeling in June 1938 and won, many Americans interpreted his victory as a symbolic defeat of Nazi Germany. This transformed Louis into a national hero even though he was Black.

Joe Louis reads about his recent victory over Tony Galento in 1939.

W. E. B. Du Bois

W. E. B. Du Bois was widely considered one of the most influential African American writers and leading male civil rights leaders of the first half of the 20th century. He wrote extensively about African American issues. One of his most famous books was *The Souls of Black Folk* (1903), in which he explained "double consciousness." Double consciousness is the idea that African Americans are always aware of two things at the same time: how they see themselves, and how the white world sees them. This idea is still talked about today. In 1909, Du Bois helped found the NAACP to work for African American civil rights, and in 1939, he released *Black Folk: Then and Now*, a history of Black Americans.

Portrait of W. E. B. Du Bois, a groundbreaking writer.

On June 28, 1939, Louis defended his title against another white man, "Two Ton" Tony Galento, and won yet again, making it clear that he would not retire his boxing gloves anytime soon. In fact, his reign as the heavyweight champion stretched for more than a decade straight, from 1937 to 1949.

Future of the African American Family

Even as athletes like Joe Louis made history, many African Americans went without having their basic needs met. Proper food and housing were a problem for a significant amount of the population. Health care was also an area where Black citizens did not have the same

A doctor gives malaria medicine to an African American family in South Carolina.

African Americans wait to receive medical care outside of a doctor's office in Mississippi.

level of access as white Americans did. However, the interests of other frequently overlooked groups, like women, would begin to impact the African American community.

Women's Equality on Hold

Although women had finally won their right to vote in 1920, and a few served in public office, these developments didn't mean there was true gender equality in the United States. Not only were women primarily restricted to a handful of jobs, such as teaching and domestic work—jobs seen as unfit for men—they were also paid much less than men.

Positive Picture Books

Librarian Augusta Baker also cared about African American families; she wanted to help mothers and children connect to literature. As a Black woman, she knew how important it was for children to see people like themselves depicted positively in the books they read. So in 1939, she curated a collection of children's books positively showing Black characters and Black culture. It was the first of its kind. The children who read these books would come of age during the civil rights movement of the 1950s and 1960s.

Augusta Baker reads to a child in 1939.

Margaret Sanger (center) in 1939.

In fact, the federal government demanded that female employees be paid 25 percent less than male employees.

African American women were particularly restricted. They had to contend with the same racist discrimination that kept their husbands out of work, while fighting the inequality that limited women's job opportunities.

Margaret Sanger

Margaret Sanger was a well-known white activist who dedicated her work to advancing women's rights. Beginning in the 1910s, Sanger had opened health clinics across the United States to give women more options when handling their health and planning their families. In Harlem, a largely Black area of New York City, the clinic she opened for Black women had an African American doctor to treat patients.

In July 1939, Sanger proposed a new project for the rural areas of the south that she called the Negro Project. In these areas, Black patients received very poor health care. There was only one hospital for every 100,000 African Americans, while white Americans had one hospital for every 19,000 people. White hospitals refused to treat Black patients. As a result, Black women were forced to rely on the poorer hospitals and health centers, or on home remedies.

Women line up outside one of Margaret Sanger's clinics in New York City.

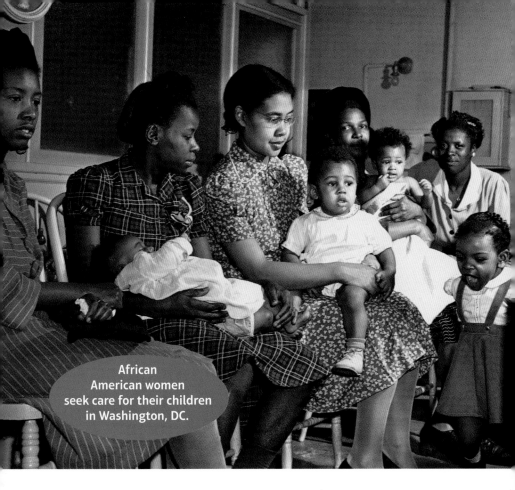

African American women seek care for their children in Washington, DC.

Sanger's project helped open more medical clinics in Black neighborhoods in the rural South, thus increasing African American women's access to health care.

To this day, however, Margaret Sanger's motivations toward the Black community remain controversial. She has been accused of being a racist who ultimately didn't want Black families to have more children. In the end, she was unable to earn the trust of the Black community, and the Negro project ended in 1942. ■

Judge Jane Bolin is the first African American female judge in the U.S.

5

A New Chapter for the NAACP

On July 22, Jane Bolin made history as the first Black female judge in the United States. The mayor of New York, Fiorello La Guardia, appointed her a judge of the Domestic Relations Court, a court that focused on helping families and children. The announcement was made at the New York City Building on the 1939 World's Fair grounds.

Although this appointment was momentous, Jane Bolin had achieved many firsts already. She was the first Black female graduate of Yale Law School, one of the top law schools in the entire country. She was also the first Black woman to join the New York City Bar Association and the New York City Bar Department, two prominent legal associations.

Two women from the NAACP meet with the wrongfully accused Scottsboro Boys in the 1930s.

During her 39-year career, Bolin focused on the rights of children, encouraging integrated services so that African American children would receive the same treatment as white children.

She also served on the boards of several organizations aimed at improving the lives of African Americans, including the Child Welfare League of America, the National Urban League, and the NAACP.

The NAACP at Work

During the 1930s, the NAACP had its hands full. It took on high-profile and racially charged criminal cases, such as that of the "Scottsboro Boys," nine Black youths who were wrongfully accused of assaulting two white women on a train. The NAACP also mounted legal cases against segregation in public schools.

The 1939 World's Fair

In 1939, more than 44 million people attended the World's Fair, a massive attraction whose slogan was "Dawn of a New Day." Promising to show visitors "the world of tomorrow," the fair showcased everything from time capsules to robots.

A world's fair isn't like a small state fair. It is a huge international exhibition where dozens of countries display their achievements. These fairs, which can continue for up to six months, began in 1791 in what is now the Czech Republic and continue to this day all over the world, from the United States to Kazakhstan to France.

At the 1939 fair in Queens, New York, dozens of countries, including Japan, France, Italy, and the Soviet Union, built massive exhibits aimed at demonstrating their commitment to world peace. Despite the growing unrest in Europe, it seemed that a better, fairer future was just around the corner.

Unfortunately, these countries would soon find themselves at war with one another.

A snapshot from the 1939 World's Fair.

And it sent an undercover writer to expose the poor working conditions of 30,000 African American employees working on the Mississippi River Flood Control Project of the War Department.

The organization was juggling criminal cases, education, segregation, and workers' rights, all at the same time.

Legal Defense Fund

Civil rights lawyer Thurgood Marshall, who worked for the Houston, Texas, chapter of the NAACP, realized that it would be more efficient and effective to divide up the NAACP's tasks. So on July 27, 1939, he outlined his plans for creating the NAACP Legal Defense Fund. This new branch of the NAACP would focus on fighting for **economic**, civil, and political rights in court.

Marshall had been associated with the NAACP for most of his law career. After graduating at the top of his class from the Howard University School of Law in 1933, he worked with the NAACP on a legal case, *Murray v. Pearson*, challenging segregation in law schools. The NAACP won the case in 1936.

Thurgood Marshall, founder of the NAACP Legal Defense Fund.

By 1938, he had joined the organization's staff and become the head of its legal department.

When Marshall founded the Legal Defense Fund in 1940, it was the first **nonprofit** agency focused on providing educational and legal aid to African Americans. It aimed to use all legal means possible to oppose Jim Crow and the "separate but equal" policies that were anything but equal.

The creation of the Legal Defense Fund marked a huge milestone for Marshall. It allowed him to concentrate on achieving constitutional and legal rights for African Americans by bringing anti-segregation cases to the Supreme Court.

The Alexandria Library

As Marshall started the Legal Defense Fund, another young African American lawyer fought segregation on a much smaller—but still very important—scale. His name was Samuel W. Tucker, and he set his sights on the public library in Alexandria, Virginia.

Alexandria's public library was an impressive place. Rows and rows of reading material filled each room. Children and adults alike could spend hours absorbed in the pages of their favorite books. The two-year-old library had already become a staple of the Alexandria community. Within its walls, knowledge was free and available to everyone.

The Alexandria Library in 1939.

Well, not *everyone*. Although African Americans had been taxed to pay for the library, they were not allowed to enter it.

In 1939, Tucker wanted to change this. He knew firsthand how important it was to be able to educate oneself in spaces like libraries. He had taught himself law instead of attending law school. At just 20 years old, he passed the Virginia bar, the difficult exam necessary to become a lawyer in the state.

As soon as Tucker learned that Alexandria's public library was shutting out African Americans, he knew he had to do something. He tried several times to legally petition the library to integrate, but these efforts never worked. He decided to use more creative means. He would organize one of the first **sit-ins** in the United States.

A Historic Sit-In

A sit-in is a peaceful protest in which people sit down and refuse to leave until their demands are met. Although this would become a popular tactic of the civil rights movement in the 1950s and 1960s, it was relatively new in 1939.

To pull it off, Tucker had to be strategic. He trained several African American men in the art of **nonviolent resistance**, including how to remain peaceful even in the face of police violence.

On August 21, the first African American protester entered the library. He politely requested a library card. The librarian denied him because he was Black.

A police officer marches five men out of the Alexandria Library after the sit-in.

Nonviolent Resistance

The tactics that Samuel W. Tucker employed in 1939 were known as nonviolent resistance, also called **civil disobedience**. This meant that activists deliberately but politely broke rules or laws that they deemed unfair, without ever becoming violent or even angry. This method was effective because it was peaceful yet radical. Other forms of nonviolent resistance included refusing to use racist institutions (boycotting) and sitting in the "whites-only" side of segregated areas.

Samuel Tucker, civil rights activist and lawyer, working at his desk.

Instead of leaving, he sat down and began to read at a table, just as the white patrons were doing.

Five minutes later, another African American man entered to request a library card. Again, the librarian refused, and this man began to study somewhere else in the library.

Three more Black men entered and followed the same steps.

Flustered and infuriated by the Black men's presence, the librarian called city hall, which alerted the police. The police told the five protesters to leave. The men politely refused three times. After the third time, the police threatened to arrest them. The protesters quietly followed an officer out of the library, making sure to remain calm as part of their nonviolent resistance training.

Three hundred onlookers had gathered around the library to watch as the officer walked the protesters out. Seeing African Americans resist Jim Crow laws in such a fashion was rare. The press picked up the story about the discrimination and the sit-in; both the *Washington Post* and the *Chicago Defender*, an African American newspaper, ran articles about the incident. However, the sit-in did not receive the nationwide media attention that Tucker had hoped for.

The five protesters were arrested and charged

A librarian stands outside of the "separate but equal" Robert Robinson Library.

with disorderly conduct. In court, their lawyer, Tucker, proved that this charge was untrue, as the men were dressed nicely and behaved well. Arguing that the library's policy was clear racism, Tucker urged the judge to rule that the library had to integrate.

Instead, the judge sided with the library. Alexandria's public library would remain segregated.

Separate and Unequal

City officials feared that similar sit-ins would happen again. To avoid this outcome, they decided to open a "separate but equal" library for African Americans as soon as possible.

The Robert Robinson Library opened its doors the following year. The building was crumbling, and the books were falling apart. The new library received worn-out hand-me-downs in the form of books and furniture from Alexandria's public library.

Tucker vowed to never enter the Robert Robinson Library. "I refuse and will always refuse," he wrote in a letter to the head librarian of the Alexandria Library, explaining why he would not get a library card from Robert Robinson.

After the sit-in, Tucker kept fighting to gain African Americans equal access to knowledge and education. He became a lawyer for the NAACP, where he applied himself to fighting segregation in schools and argued more than 50 civil rights cases.

It would be 20 more years until the public library in Alexandria was integrated. ▪

The Nazi Party on the rise in 1939.

6

War in Europe

As African Americans slowly made advancements in the United States, such as gaining the right to serve in the Air Force and founding civil rights organizations, something terrible and frightening was happening overseas.

On September 1, 1939, Nazi Germany invaded the country of Poland, breaking an international treaty and killing thousands of people. The leader of Nazi Germany, Adolf Hitler, imprisoned all Jewish people. After taking control of Poland, the Nazis built **concentration camps**, where they would torture and kill millions of Jews and others. This was called the **Holocaust**.

On September 3, France and Britain declared war on Germany. They saw the evil acts that Hitler was committing and felt that it was their duty to protect the European Jews, as well as their own borders. This was the beginning of World War II.

Staying Neutral

Congress and the American people were not as eager to intervene. Nazi Germany's treatment of Jews and other minorities was terrible, but since it was happening across the Atlantic, in Europe, it was considered a European problem.

At that time, the official stance of the U.S. government was that America needed to focus on American issues. Americans were still struggling to escape the Great Depression, and they felt they had to take care of their own country before they could extend help to anyone else.

On September 5, President Roosevelt officially declared neutrality. This meant the United States would stay out of the war.

An isolationist image urges Americans to stay out of the war.

The U.S. refused to accept a ship with Jewish refugees who escaped Nazi Germany.

Isolationism

An October 6 poll found that most Americans agreed with the president. They did not want to send troops to fight against Nazi Germany, preferring to focus on issues directly threatening America. This point of view was called **isolationism**.

However, not all Americans agreed with this outlook. African Americans and Jewish Americans had reason to be skeptical.

Historically, African Americans and Jews found common ground because both had faced discrimination in the United States. Jewish professors banned from white universities often taught at historically Black colleges and universities, such as Howard. And when Black customers were refused service at whites-only stores, Jewish shopkeepers would typically serve them.

The U.S. Senate Post Office in Washington, DC, is flooded with letters from American citizens reacting to the issue of neutrality.

The concept of isolationism was complicated. On the one hand, the majority of Americans seemed to be sending a clear message: They didn't care about protecting racial minorities in the United States, and they didn't care about protecting religious minorities abroad.

On the other hand, many Americans who supported isolationism had fought in World War I or had lost family members and friends in World War I, and they did not want to repeat the past. More than 115,000 Americans had died in that war. There was no telling how many might die in another one.

Cash-and-Carry

Some Americans saw isolationism as a purely economic issue. They were still reeling from the Great Depression and were hesitant to join what would undoubtedly be an expensive war. The U.S. government, however, soon realized that the country could make money off the war while technically staying out of it. In early November, despite American neutrality, Roosevelt signed a new policy enacted by Congress at his request: "cash-and-carry."

This allowed countries such as Britain and France to purchase American weapons—as long as they paid in cash and transported the weapons themselves. This allowed the United States to technically stay neutral while still profiting from the sale of weapons. The policy would later be replaced by the Lend-Lease Act in early 1941. Instead of selling arms and supplies for cash, the United States would lend and lease supplies, on credit, to countries that were fighting Nazi Germany and were therefore "vital to the defense of the United States."

Cash-and-carry benefited Americans economically. Factories began to increase production to meet

English soldiers unload weapons they received from the U.S.

Women work at a weapons factory.

the surging demand for arms. The increase in production meant an increase in the need for workers.

The Depression Ends

Weapon production created thousands of jobs, which greatly improved the American economy. At long last, the Great Depression was truly ending—at least for white Americans.

Because most factories continued their decades-old policy of hiring only white workers, this economic recovery did not reach the majority of African Americans. They still had a great deal of trouble finding employment, and even when they could, they were still forced to do the unwanted and lowest-paying jobs.

But more and more African American labor activists were determined to fight this discrimination.

African Americans in Labor Unions

Labor unions—organizations that protected and promoted workers' rights—were largely privileges that only white people could access. Many labor unions refused to accept Black members, and it wasn't uncommon to see white workers attempt to drive Black workers out of jobs. A labor union called the Brotherhood of Sleeping Car Porters, founded by A. Philip Randolph, started in the 1920s. Sleeping car porters were workers who shined shoes, carried suitcases, and catered to white passengers in overnight trains, which were called "sleeping cars." This was the first predominantly African American labor union. Others followed. It wasn't until 1939, when World War II and the cash-and-carry policy sparked an increase in factory production, that white labor unions finally began to integrate. For the first time, many African American and white workers found themselves working side by side at the same factories.

A. Philip Randolph (first row, third from left) leads the Brotherhood of Sleeping Car Porters.

Black Americans and Boeing

After the introduction of the cash-and-carry policy, one of the companies that began increasing its production was the Boeing Airplane Company, based in Seattle, Washington. It was one of the largest aircraft producers in the United States, manufacturing 28 percent of all the aircraft in the country, and would therefore have to lead the way in wartime production. During the six-year war, Boeing built nearly 100,000 aircraft.

Even though Seattle was in the North, which was less segregated than the South, the company's founder, William E. Boeing, echoed Jim Crow sentiments by refusing to employ African Americans.

The Boeing Airplane Company starts increasing the production of bomber planes in 1939.

Beginning in November 1939, African American labor rights activists fought to change this fact.

Reporter Hutchen R. Hutchins organized Black workers into the Committee for the Defense of Negro Labor's Right to Work at the Boeing Airplane Company. Together, they pressured the company to hire them.

Hutchins also began reporting on Boeing's unfair hiring practices for the *Northwest Enterprise*, Seattle's African American newspaper. Spotlighting Boeing's racial discrimination for the whole country to see, Hutchins's articles helped bring federal attention to the issue.

In June 1941, Executive Order 8802 from President Roosevelt finally banned racial discrimination at any companies that did work for the government. This included Boeing. It would be another year, however, before the company hired the first Black employees in its 26-year history.

Gone with the Wind

African Americans weren't making room for themselves just in factories; they were also making room for themselves on the big screen. On December 15, the film *Gone with the Wind* was released to wide critical acclaim. It set records for the most Oscar wins, as well as the highest profits for any film.

African American actress Butterfly McQueen appears in *Gone with the Wind.*

The film was a love story about a slave owner who loses her plantation during the Civil War. Although white audiences loved the film, many African Americans did not, because it glorified slavery and depicted its African American characters as unintelligent. For example, many of the slaves in the movie seemed happy to be enslaved—which, historically, could not be further from the truth.

From Spirituals to Swing

While *Gone with the Wind* depicted African Americans in **stereotyped** ways, white record producer and activist John Hammond wanted to depict Black culture as it really was. And he wanted to do it at New York City's Carnegie Hall, one of the world's most famous stages.

Hattie McDaniel

The first African American to ever win an Oscar was Hattie McDaniel, who played an enslaved woman called Mammy in *Gone with the Wind*. At the film's release, many African Americans became upset that her role in the film promoted Black stereotypes. In response, she said, "Why should I complain about making $700 a week playing a maid? If I didn't, I'd be making $7 a week being one."

McDaniel had already begun making a name for herself as early as 1924, when she became one the first African Americans to sing on the radio in the United States.

Over the course of her career, she appeared in more than 300 films, despite widespread prejudice against Black performers. In 1975, she was inducted into the Black Filmmakers Hall of Fame.

Hattie McDaniel accepts her Oscar in 1940 for her role in in the 1939 film, *Gone with the Wind*.

He organized a concert called From Spirituals to Swing. The show celebrated the history of Black music, tracing its development from the Black spirituals of the 18th century all the way to the swing music popular in the 1930s. He had organized a similar concert in December 1938. It was such a hit that he decided to bring it back on December 24, 1939, bigger and better than ever.

In addition to celebrating African American culture, the concert shined the spotlight on African American artists. It featured performances from legendary musicians such as Big Joe Turner, a singer whose work heavily inspired early rock 'n' roll. Other headliners were pianist and composer James P. Johnson and singer Helen Humes, a defining figure of swing music. "King of Swing" Benny Goodman

The Count Basie Orchestra plays in From Spirituals to Swing.

A sound recording of From Spirituals to Swing.

and his band also performed. Goodman was not African American, but as a Jewish man, he was no stranger to discrimination, and his inclusion in the show further highlighted the strong ties between the African American and Jewish American communities.

From Spirituals to Swing was a momentous opportunity for Black artists to go onstage at the world-famous Carnegie Hall. Just a few months earlier, Marian Anderson had been denied access to Constitution Hall, but now legendary Black artists would be showcased on America's most prestigious concert stage. And the audience was integrated. ■

Four African American men in the South have been imprisoned and forced to work.

The Legacy of 1939 in Civil Rights History

The year 1939 was a historic one for civil rights.

The Black Cabinet made sure the president took African American communities into account. The founding of the CLU demonstrated that the federal government was ready to start working toward ensuring the civil rights of Black citizens.

Marian Anderson's historic rendition of "My Country, 'Tis of Thee" briefly brought the country together and proved that an integrated future could be possible.

Jane Bolin became the first African American judge in the United States, and the NAACP Legal Defense Fund laid the groundwork for landmark legal battles to come. For the first time since the end of the Civil War, lawyers were positioned to strike down Jim Crow laws and end segregation.

Activists involved in the Alexandria Library sit-in and in rising Black labor movements began to perfect the nonviolent resistance that would define the civil rights movement over the next three decades.

And while films like *Gone with the Wind* stereotyped African Americans, their positive representation in librarian Augusta Baker's curated children's book collection and in John Hammond's From Spirituals to Swing showed that Black culture was worth celebrating.

Across the ocean, Germany's march through Europe continued. Although it started on that continent, the conflict quickly grew to engulf the entire globe.

The United States managed to dodge the war in 1939, first with isolationism, then with its cash-and-carry policy and later its lend-lease program, but the country would not be able to isolate forever. As

more and more weapons were produced, it became increasingly clear that American soldiers would soon have to take up arms. A long, hard-fought war awaited the United States.

At the same time, the country still had a long way to go in protecting the civil rights of all its citizens. During World War I, African Americans had been willing to fight in segregated units, but it was now a new era. If the nation wanted Black soldiers to fight for freedom overseas, they would have to start gaining freedom at home in America. That meant an end to segregation, an end to Jim Crow, and an end to "separate but equal." Black Americans would need to be treated—finally—as equals.

Was America ready? ■

African American protestors unite against Jim Crow in Philadelphia, Pennsylvania, in 1948.

Stacey Abrams

Stacey Yvonne Abrams was born on December 9, 1973, the second of six children. She was born in Wisconsin but raised in Mississippi, and over the course of her political career, she has campaigned tirelessly for voter rights in the South.

Even in her youth, Abrams had a heart for civil rights and politics. Her parents taught her the importance of voting and took her to do volunteer work at prisons and polling places. She became a speechwriter for a congressional campaign at just 17 years old.

As a student at the historically Black women's school Spelman

Stacey Abrams sits in the State Capitol in Atlanta, Georgia, in 2017.

College, she interned at the Environmental Protection Agency and worked in the office of the mayor in Atlanta, Georgia. She graduated with high honors in 1995 and went on to earn a Doctor of Laws degree from Yale Law School in 1998.

Her political career began in 2002 when, at 29 years old, she was appointed a deputy city attorney in Atlanta. In 2006, she was elected to the Georgia House of Representatives as a Democrat. In 2010, she became the first African American House minority leader in the history of Georgia. Abrams served her state in its House

Stacey Abrams at age seven.

In 2013, she launched a nonprofit, the New Georgia Project, to focus on increasing voter registration, helping as many Americans as possible to make their voices heard in government. Within its first year, the organization registered 69,000 voters. By 2019, it had registered nearly 500,000. Many of those who registered were people of color—people whose voices had historically not been heard.

of Representatives for 11 years and was the Democratic leader of the House for seven of them.

Stacey Abrams speaks in the Georgia House of Representatives in 2012.

" *We are strongest when we see the most vulnerable in our society, bear witness to their struggles, and then work to create systems to make it better.*"

—STACEY ABRAMS

In 2018, the Democratic Party of Georgia nominated Abrams as its pick to run for governor. She was the first Black woman in U.S. history to become a major party's nominee for governor. Although she lost the election, there was reason to believe that the opposing candidate had engaged in voter suppression, particularly trying to disqualify thousands of registered minorities from voting.

This injustice drove her to launch Fair Fight in 2019, an organization to protect voters' rights, increase voter registration, and give a voice to as many people as possible. In addition to educating voters about their rights, Fair Fight works to ensure fair elections, not only in Georgia but across the United States.

Stacey Abrams campaigns for soon-to-be President Joe Biden before the 2020 election.

In 2019, Abrams also became the first African American woman to deliver a response to a president's State of the Union address.

For her work, Abrams has become known around the country as a symbol for voting rights. It's estimated that, leading up to the 2020 presidential election, she was responsible for 800,000 new registered voters in Georgia.

Stacey Abrams continues to work hard for every single voter today. ∎

TIMELINE

The Year in Civil Rights

1939

JANUARY 13

Members of the Black Cabinet meet to advise President Roosevelt.

FEBRUARY

Frank Murphy establishes the Civil Liberties Unit to fight for the rights of minorities.

APRIL 9

Marian Anderson sings to a crowd of thousands at the Lincoln Memorial.

APRIL 20

African American singer Billie Holiday records "Strange Fruit," which becomes a protest song against lynching.

MAY 16

The Food Stamp Program launches to help Americans put food on their tables.

JUNE 28

Joe Louis defends his heavyweight champion title against "Two Ton" Tony Galento.

JULY 22

Judge Jane Bolin is appointed as the first African American female judge in the U.S.

SEPTEMBER 1

Nazi Germany invades Poland, starting World War II.

JULY 27

Thurgood Marshall outlines his plans for creating the NAACP Legal Defense Fund.

NOVEMBER

African American labor rights activists begin to fight against Boeing Airplane Company's policy of refusing to hire Black workers.

AUGUST 21

Samuel Tucker carries out one of the first sit-ins at the Alexandria Library in Virginia.

DECEMBER 24

John Hammond organizes a second From Spirituals to Swing concert to celebrate the history of Black music.

GLOSSARY

activist (AK-tuh-vist) a person who works to bring about political or social change

amendment (uh-MEND-muhnt) a change that is made to a law or legal document

bigotry (BIG-uh-tree) dislike or hatred of a group of people based only on their identity

citizenship (SIT-i-zuhn-ship) the legal status of being a citizen of a country, with full rights to live, work, and vote there

civil disobedience (SIV-uhl dis-uh-BEE-dee-uhnce) the refusal to observe certain laws, as a peaceful form of protest

civil rights (SIV-uhl rites) the individual rights that all members of a democratic society have to freedom and equal treatment under the law

concentration camp (kahn-suhn-TRAY-shuhn kamp) a place where large numbers of people are detained or confined under armed guard

criminalize (KRIM-uh-nuhl-ize) to make a law against an action

discrimination (dis-krim-uh-NAY-shuhn) prejudice or unfair behavior to others based on differences such as race, gender, or age

domestic (duh-MES-tik) of or having to do with the home

economic (ek-uh-NAH-mik) of or having to do with the economy, which is the system of buying, selling, making things, and managing money in a society

economist (i-KAH-nuh-mist) a person who is trained in economics

federal (FED-ur-uhl) national government, as opposed to state or local government

Great Depression (grayt di-PRESH-uhn) the economic catastrophe in the United States that began in 1929 and continued through the 1930s

Holocaust (HAH-luh-kawst) the killing of millions of European Jews and others by the Nazis during World War II

integration (in-ti-GRAY-shuhn) the act or practice of making facilities or an organization open to people of all races and ethnic groups

isolationism (eye-suh-LAY-shuhn-iz-uhm) an international political policy where one country refuses to interact with other countries

Jim Crow (jim kro) the practice of segregating Black people in the United States, named after a character who degraded African American life and culture

Ku Klux Klan (KOO kluks KLAN) a secret organization in the United States that uses threats and violence to achieve its goal of white supremacy; also called the Klan or the KKK

lynching (LIN-ching) a sometimes public murder by a group of people, often involving hanging

mutiny (MYOO-tuh-nee) a revolt against or refusal to obey authority

Nazi (NAHT-see) a racist German political party that believed that white people, especially white Germans, were better than everyone else in the world; the party lasted from 1919 to 1945

nonprofit (nahn-PRAH-fit) not created or maintained for the purpose of making money

nonviolent resistance (nahn-VYE-uh-luhnt ri-ZIS-tuhns) the pursuit of social change through peaceful political actions

prejudice (PREJ-uh-dis) immovable, unreasonable, or unfair opinion about someone based on the person's race, religion, or other characteristic

prosecute (PRAH-si-kyoot) to begin and carry out legal action in a court of law against a person accused of a crime

segregation (seg-ruh-GAY-shuhn) the act or practice of keeping people or groups apart

sit-in (SIT-in) a form of protest in which demonstrators occupy a place, refusing to leave until their demands are met

Social Security (SOH-shuhl si-KYOOR-i-tee) a U.S. government program that pays money to retired and disabled people

stereotype (STARE-ee-oh-tipe) a false but popular belief or assumption about an entire group of people

testify (TES-tuh-fye) to state what you have witnessed or what you know in a court of law

voter suppression (VOH-tur suh-PRESH-uhn) preventing a certain group of people from being able to vote

BIBLIOGRAPHY

Alexandria Library. "Alexandria Library Sit-In." Last modified October 2021, https://alexlibraryva.org/1939-sit-in.

Davenport, Sarah. "Battle at Boeing: African Americans and the Campaign for Jobs 1939–1942." Seattle Civil Rights and Labor History Project, University of Washington, 2006, https://depts.washington.edu/civilr/boeing_battle.htm.

Franklin D. Roosevelt Presidential Library and Museum. "Eleanor Roosevelt and the Tuskegee Airmen." https://www.fdrlibrary.org/tuskegee.

History.com editors. "Great Depression History." HISTORY, A&E Television Networks. October 29, 2009, Last modified October 5, 2021. https://www.history.com/topics/great-depression/great-depression-history.

Matthews, Tom. "A Year in History: 1939 Timeline." Historic Newspapers. Last modified December 24, 2020, https://www.historic-newspapers.com/blog/a-year-in-history-1939-timeline/.

Thurgood Marshall (left) prepares for a segregation case in 1935.

INDEX

Abrams, Stacey, 84–85, *85*, 86, *86*, 87, *87*
Alexandria Library, 59–60, *60*, 61, *61*, 63–65, 81
Amistad mutiny, 26, *26*, 27
Anderson, Marian
  and Constitution Hall ban, 36–37, *37*, 38, 79
  Lincoln Memorial performance, 7, 32–34, *32–33*, 40, 41, 43, 81
  as world-famous performer, 32–34, *34*, 35, 41

Baker, Augusta, 50, *50*, 82
Bethune, Mary McLeod, 13, *13*
Black artists, 33–38, 50, 76–79, 82
Black Cabinet, *10*, 11, *11*, 12–14, 44, 81
Boeing Airplane Company, 74, *74*, 75
Bolin, Jane, *54*, 55–56, 81
boxing, 45–46, 48
Brotherhood of Sleeping Car Porters, 73, *73*

Cash-and-carry policy, 70, 71, *71*, 73–74, 82
Cinqué, Joseph, 26, *26*, 27
civil disobedience, 62
civil liberties, 19–23, *23*, 24
Civil Liberties Unit (CLU), 7, *18*, 20–25, 81
concentration camps, 67
Constitution Hall, 36–38
Count Basie Orchestra, *78*

Daughters of the American Revolution (DAR), 37, *37*, 38
Department of Justice (DOJ), 7, 19–20, *24*
discrimination
  against Black artists, 33–38
  and the fight for civil liberties, 19–20
  against Jewish Americans, 69, 79
  and voter suppression, 21–22
double consciousness, 47
Du Bois, W. E. B., 47, *47*

Ellington, Duke, 36, *36*
employment discrimination, 12, 51, 72–75

Fair Fight, 87
Federal Bureau of Investigation (FBI), 25, *25*
Federal Surplus Commodities Corporation, *42*, 43
Fifteenth Amendment (1870), 5, 12, 20
Food Stamp Program (FSP), 44–45
Fourteenth Amendment (1868), 5, 20
From Spirituals to Swing, 78, *78*, 79, *79*, 82

Galento, Tony, *46*, 48
Gone with the Wind, 75–76, *76*, 77, *77*, 82
Goodman, Benny, 78–79
Great Depression
  and New Deal programs, 10–11, *12*, 14
  poverty during, 7, *7*, 12, 44–45, *45*, 48
  unemployment during, 12, *12*, 43
  weapons production during, 71–72
  women workers in, 17, *72*

Hammond, John, 76, 82
health care, 48, *48*, 49, 51–52, 53, *53*, 56
Hitler, Adolf, 67
Holiday, Billie, 39, *39*
Holocaust, 67
Humes, Helen, 78
Hutchins, Hutchen R., 75

integration, 30
isolationism, 69–70, 82

Jews, 9, 67–69, *69*, 79
Jim Crow laws
  and employment discrimination, 74–75
  and justice rights, 19
  legal battles against, 6, 81
  protests against, 63–64, *82–83*
  in the South, 5–6, 19, 21–22
  and voting rights, 21–22

Johnson, James P., 78

Ku Klux Klan (KKK), 6, 53

La Guardia, Fiorello, 55
labor rights, 73–75
Lend-Lease Act, 71, 82
Louis, Joe, 46, *46*, 48
lynchings, 6, 14–15, *21*, *22*

Marshall, Thurgood, 58, *58*, 59
McDaniel, Hattie, 77, *77*
McQueen, Butterfly, *76*
Meeropol, Abel, 39
Murphy, Frank, *18*, 20

NAACP Legal Defense Fund, 7, 58–59, 81
National Association for the Advancement of Colored People (NAACP), 6, 47, 56, *56*, 58
National Association of Colored Women's Clubs (NACWC), 6
Nazi Germany, 9, 31, 46, *66*, 67–68, 71, 82
Negro Project, 52–53
New Deal, 10, *12*, 14
nonviolent resistance, 61–63, 82

Plessy v. Ferguson (1896), 6

Randolph, A. Philip, 73, *73*
Robert Robinson Library, *64*, 65
Roosevelt, Eleanor, 14–15, *15*, 38, *38*
Roosevelt, Franklin Delano
and Black airmen, 31
and the Black Cabinet, *10*, 11, *11*, 12–13, 81
cash-and-carry policy, *71*
and decline of support for anti-lynching bill, 15
and Marion Anderson performance, 41
and neutrality in World War II, 10, 68, 71
and New Deal programs, 10, 14, 44
and racial discrimination ban, 75
State of the Union address, *8*, 9

Sanger, Margaret, 51–53, *51*, *52*
Schmeling, Max, 46
Scottsboro Boys, 56, *56*
segregation
and Black artists, 33–38
in labor unions, 73
NAACP Legal Defense Fund and, 58–59
and nonviolent resistance, 62–64
in public schools, *4*, 56, 65
in sports, 45
in the U.S. military, 29–31, *82*, 83, *83*
sit-ins, 60–61, 63–65
Social Security, 15–16
South
discrimination in court cases, 23–25
Jim Crow laws in, 5–6, 19, 21–22
lynchings in, 15
voting discrimination in, 21–22, 86–87

Tappan, Lewis, 27, *27*
Thirteenth Amendment (1865), 5, 20
Tucker, Samuel W., 59–62, *62*, 64–65
Turner, Big Joe, 78

Van Buren, Martin, 27
voter suppression, 21–22, 29, 87
voting rights, 6, 20, *20*, 21–22, 84, 86–87

Women, 16–17, *17*, 49, 51–53, *53*
Works Progress Administration (WPA), 14
World War I, *28*, 29–30, *30*, 31
World War II
cash-and-carry policy, 71, *71*, 73–74
and Nazi Germany, 9, 31, 46, 67–68, 71, 82
U.S. involvement in, 10, 68, *68*, 69–70, 82–83
weapons production during, 71, *71*, 72, *72*, 74, 83
World's Fair (1939), 55, 57, *57*

About the Author

Jay Leslie is a writer who cares about revolution. Her other books include *Who Did It First? 50 Politicians, Activists and Entrepreneurs Who Revolutionized the World* and *Game, Set, Sisters! The Story of Venus and Serena Williams.* Connect with Jay at www.Jay-Leslie.com.

PHOTO CREDITS